I CAN CALM MY MIND

Written by Amber Raymond & Lynn McLaughlin

Illustrated by Allysa Batin

Illustrated by Allysa Batin

ISBN: 978-1-7388582-2-4 (paperback)
ISBN: 978-1-7780741-5-8 (ebook)

Printed by Print Works
382 Devonshire Road
Windsor, Ontario N8Y 2L4

https://lynnmclaughlin.com
https://www.directconnections.ca

We all feel many emotions as a part of life experience. The positive and negative feelings can help us understand ourselves and the world around us.

The characters on the planet Tezra glow in the following colours to match how they are feeling.

<u>Red</u>	<u>Orange</u>	<u>Blue</u>	<u>Yellow</u>	<u>Green</u>	<u>Purple</u>
Anger	Scared	Sad	Surprised	Happy	Lonely
Frustration	Worried	Disappoint-ed	Unexpected Event	1 Believe in Myself	
	Uncertain				

Are You Up For A Challenge?

- Can you tell by the look on their faces, by body language or the words they are using? Maybe you can tell by the colour of their glow. Can you see how your friends are feeling just by looking at them?

- Have you ever felt the same way? How do you express your own feelings?

They didn't want me.

They don't think
I'm good enough.

I don't fit in.

"Hey Carnuli, I'm just checking in," Trine said, lightly knocking on the door of the bedroom.

"I can't fall asleep."

"What's up?" Trine asked.

"Did something happen today that made you feel **sad**? I heard you crying and I can see from your blue glow and the tears in your eyes that you are **sad** or **disappointed**."

"Yeah, you're right. I am **sad**." Carnuli realized.

Trine asked, "Why do you think you're **sad** Carnuli"?
"Yes, I can understand why you would be **disappointed**," said Trine.

"I saw all my friends playing at the park without me. They didn't even tell me they were going."

Trine then asked, "Would you like to tell me what you're thinking about?"

"Well... maybe they don't like me."

"Maybe they just forgot about me."

"Maybe they didn't want me there."

"Maybe they think I'm annoying."

"I would find it hard to fall asleep too with all those **sad** thoughts in my head. Can I teach you something that helps me to calm my mind when I have **sad** thoughts?" Trine asked.

"Yeah, I'd like that," said Carnuli.

"It's called taking full breaths. You breathe in for the same amount of time that you breathe out with a pause in the middle. Let me show you how."
INHALE

EXHALE

"Start by closing your eyes. Now inhale through your nose for one Tezrania, two Tezrania, three Tezrania."
ONE TEZRANIA

TWO TEZRANIA
THREE TEZRANIA
"Now pause."

"Exhale through your mouth for one Tezrania, two Tezrania, three Tezrania."
ONE TEZRANIA

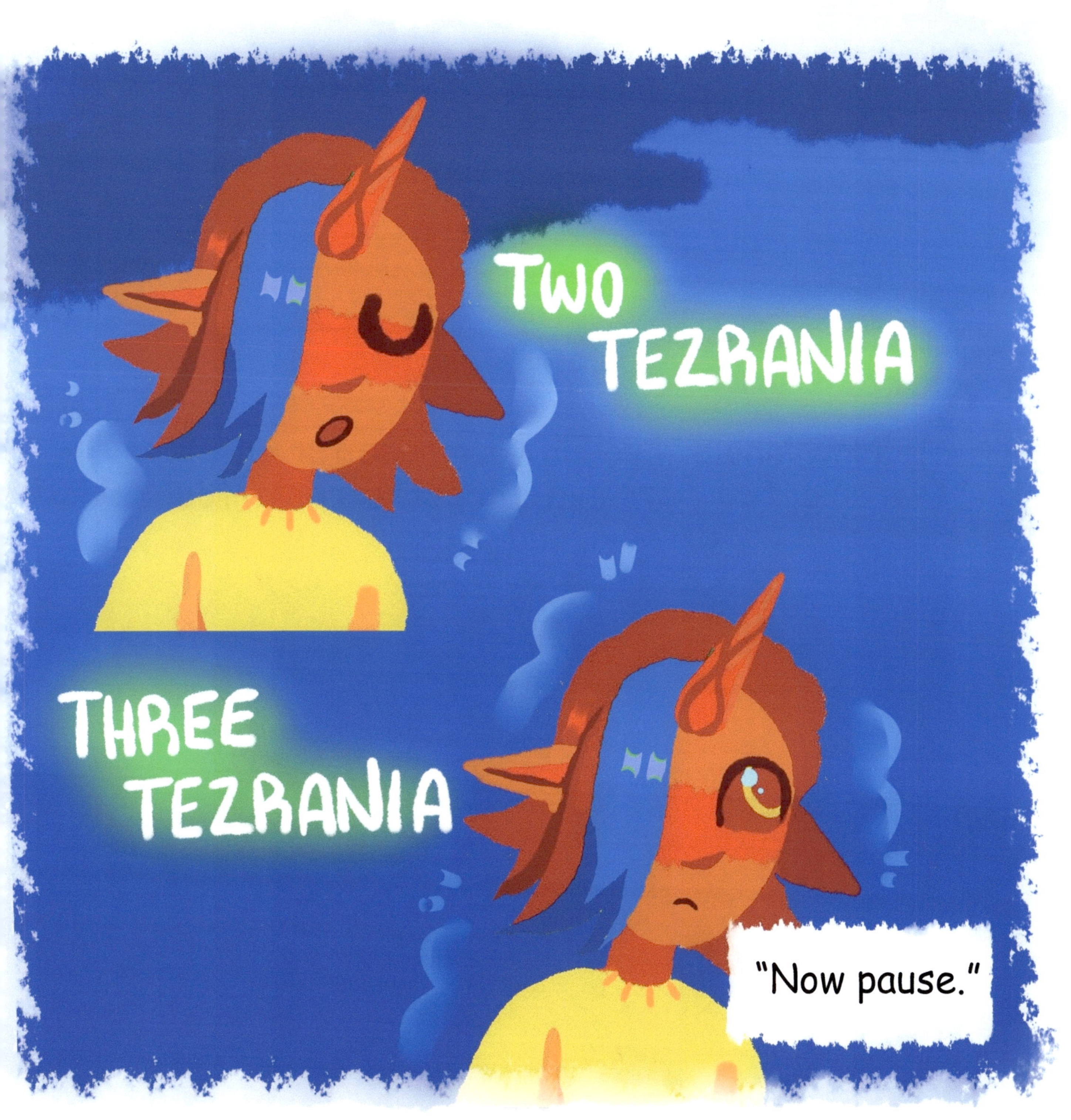
TWO TEZRANIA
THREE TEZRANIA
"Now pause."

"Now inhale through your nose for one Tezrania, two Tezrania, three Tezrania, four Tezrania, and pause."
ONE TEZRANIA
TWO TEZRANIA

"Oh, the air going in
my nose is cold."

"Exhale through your mouth for one Tezrania, two Tezrania, three Tezrania, four Tezrania. Now pause."

"The breath going out is warm on my lips."

"Inhale through your nose for one Tezrania, two Tezrania, three Tezrania, four Tezrania, five Tezrania. Now pause."
ONE
TWO
THREE
FOUR
FIVE

"My heart is beating slower!"

"Exhale through your mouth for one Tezrania, two Tezrania, three Tezrania, four Tezrania, five Tezrania. Now pause."

"Wow, I don't have as many **sad** thoughts!"

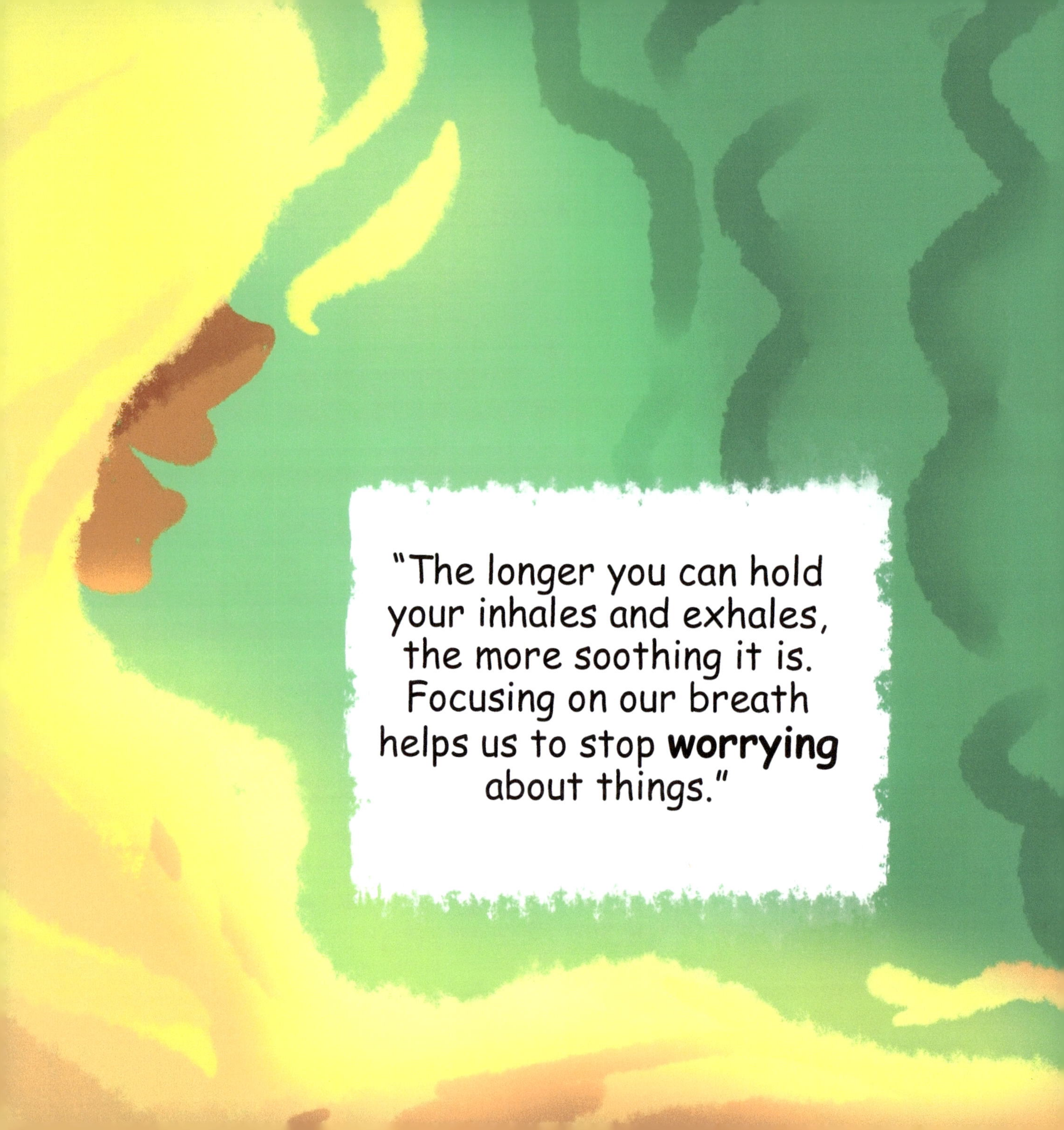

"The longer you can hold
your inhales and exhales,
the more soothing it is.
Focusing on our breath
helps us to stop **worrying**
about things."

"It really helped me to feel **calm**. Thanks Trine!" Carnuli said. "I bet I can inhale and exhale for 8 seconds next time!"

"Yeah, let's try it out!" Trine agreed.

"Thank you Trine. I'll remember to breathe like that the next time I feel **sad**. Perhaps my friends had a reason why I wasn't invited. I'll talk to them about it tomorrow."

Sometimes when we have big emotions, our thoughts can play tricks on us.

Thankfully, You Can Calm Your Mind Too!

1. Notice that your thoughts are stopping you from doing something you want to do.

2. Name the way you're feeling.

3. Make yourself comfortable so you won't be distracted.

4. Close your eyes. Now inhale and exhale for the same amount of time.

5. Continue inhaling and exhaling, increasing the length of each breath.

6. Ask yourself how you are feeling now.

"I can calm my mind."

"I can check my senses."
"I can ground myself."

Vocabulary

Inhale - To breathe in through your nose

Exhale - To breathe out through your mouth

Full Breaths - Inhaling and exhaling at a slow, counted pace to help calm ourselves

Soothing - Making
ourselves feel calm
and comfortable

Disappointed - How
we feel when something
doesn't go as we expected

Like You, Every Crystal is Unique!

Did you notice the characters are all named after crystals?

Some crystals look like simple rocks, and others look like they're from another planet. No matter their appearance, they all make you feel a sense of wonder when you see the way they shine.

Also known as rocks, gemstones, and minerals, crystals are formed through geological processes by heat and pressure underground. Working with crystals can help you transform into the most powerful version of yourself by guiding you to see how incredible you truly are.

Carnelian (*Carnuli*): empowerment, focus, action and confidence

Citrine (Trine) empowerment, confidence, creativity, manifestation and abundance

Lapis Lazuli (*Lazu*): intuition, education, communication and problem solving

Epidote (Epido): energize, healthy, strengthen, provide hope, open you to love and joy

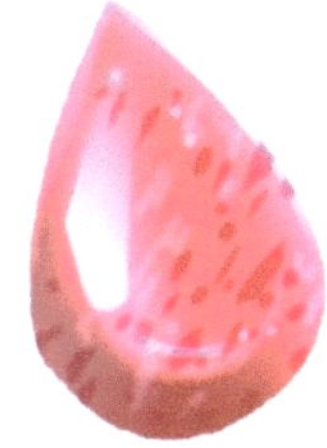

Zircon (Zirco) : Confidence, wisdom, love and happiness

Amber Raymond

BA, BSW, MSW, RSW

WWW.DIRECTCONNECTIONS.CA

As a Social Worker, Amber is an advocate for unconventional, evidence-based coping strategies and is devoted to her friends and family.

She is passionate about child mental health, lifelong self-care practices, self-exploration, self-love, and holistic wellbeing.

When not practicing social work, Amber likes to research new, effective methods to overcoming life's mental and emotional challenges.

Lynn McLaughlin

MED, BED, BA

WWW.LYNNMCLAUGHLIN.COM

Lynn McLaughlin served as a Superintendent of Education, Administrator and Teacher. Lynn continues to be active in education, teaching future Educational Assistants at her local college.

Lynn hosts the inspirational podcast "Taking the Helm" which can be found on your favourite podcast app. It's another way to learn more about children's well-being.

As a best-selling, award-winning author, and Rotarian, Lynn is dedicated to community causes and volunteerism.

Allysa Batin

Allysa Batin is a young freelance illustrator. She enjoys creating fun and colourful characters and advocating for love and acceptance in her art.

She's happy to spread positivity through the book series.

Scan the code for your free follow up resources to help readers learn and practice the strategy.

What other adventures do these friends find themselves in?

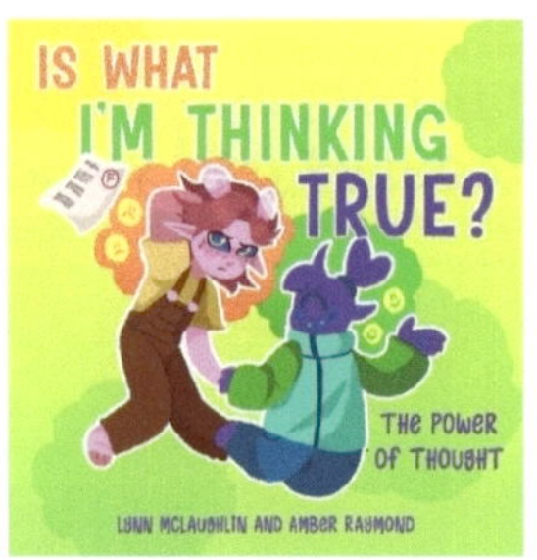

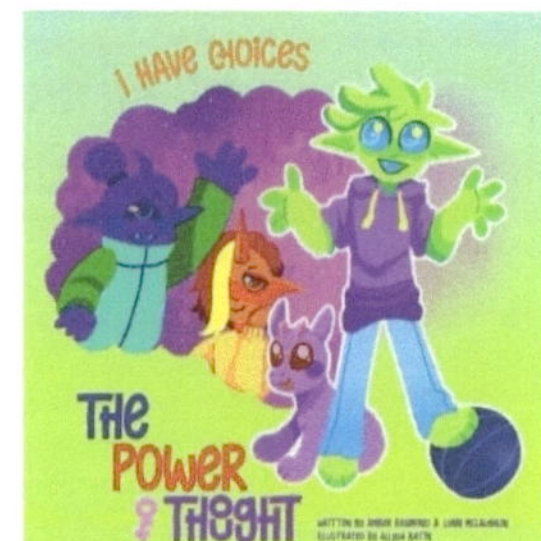

www.thepowerofthought.ca